A JOURNEY WITH SIBBEL

An 18th-Century
Orphan's Study
of Needlework

Susan Greening Davis
and Sally Criswell

A JOURNEY WITH SIBBEL

An 18th-Century Orphan's Study of Needlework

By Susan Greening Davis and Sally Criswell

Editor: Stacey A. Fischkelta
Designer: Bob Deck
Photography: Aaron T. Leimkuehler
Illustration: Eric Sears
Original Charts: Penny Conway
Cross Stitch Chart Creator: Alissa Christianson
Technical Editor: Mary Atherton
Photo Editor: Jo Ann Groves

Published by:
Kansas City Star Books
1729 Grand Blvd.
Kansas City, Missouri, USA 64108

ISBN: 978-1-61169-157-3
Library of Congress Control Number: 2014960078

Printed in the United States of America by Walsworth Publishing Co., Marceline, MO
To order bulk copies, call StarInfo at (816) 234-4473; to order single copies, call (816) 234-4242.

Star Stitch
THE KANSAS CITY STAR

Acknowledgments

We would like to take this opportunity to thank the following friends, without whose work and support this adventure would not have happened:

Penny Conway for all of the set-ups and graphic work.

Brenda Parkhurst, Shina Lyons, Bonnie Mauk, Marketta Steck and Michelle Estes for help with stitching samples.

The Gentle Art, Weeks Dye Works, and Wichelt Imports, who furnished supplies for the samples.

Mary Atherton of Old Mill Stitchery, for allowing us to use her beautiful shop for the photo shoot. Her shop is part of the Corbin Mill Place, 131 S. Water St. in Liberty, Missouri.

Sandy, for letting us wander throughout her shop and the five other shops housed in her historical building.

Edie McGinnis and Aaron Leimkuehler. I had "the time of my life" doing Sibbel's photo shoot! Your expertise and fellowship let me relax and enjoy every minute. It was over too soon, Susan.

And our editor, Stacey Fischkelta, for her help and support.

Old Mill Stitchery

About the Authors

First, we must dedicate this book to our stitcher, Sibbel. She brought us to this journey.

It is difficult to dedicate something like this without acknowledging the two people who made this possible for *all* of us, Ken and Ginnie Thompson. They are the reason that the beautiful art of counted thread cross stitch was brought to America, from Denmark, and we have been loving every stitch since. Unfortunately, they are both gone now, but their love of the craft, and their teaching lives on.

Ken and Ginnie believed in me when I owned two needlework shops. They believed in me as an educator, and submitted me to study my first foreign class in Denmark with the Baroness and her assistant. Since then I have been invited for private study in Italy, England, Spain, Germany, Ireland, and France. Sally Criswell has accompanied me on many of these extraordinary opportunities. What a whirlwind of learning needlework history it has been. I offer a thank you to all of those past embroiderers who loved a technique that became known in their region. My mission is to keep sharing these techniques and the love I have of them with you.

When DMC awarded me an International Teaching Award, I realized that teaching needlework and its historical importance was something that needed to continue. I have been fortunate to educate a parade of students over the years.

I have also had the opportunity to represent our industry on Home and Garden Television (HGTV) twice, bringing many more followers to our loved counted thread cross stitch.

My "Susan's Groupies," (I *did not* set this up!) and chatroom members have been faithful followers to all of the traveling adventures and weekend retreats. Many have been with me for 40 years and are still stitching!

My husband, CJ, has taken me to and from airports to travel all over this beautiful United States and Europe. He went on one Alaskan cruise and learned right away that I was there for my stitchers. That is what has been in my heart since I started my journey, more than 40 years ago: to be there for all stitchers, beginners to advanced.

Thank you, all.
Still Stitching, Susan

As a child, I learned to crochet one summer while staying with my grandmother in Chicago. I did not realize that at night she would pull out my stitches and re-wind the ball saying that I needed to work on my tension. (We only had the one ball of yarn.)

I learned to do counted cross stitch from a wonderful Girl Scout leader who was so patient with me. Little did I know then that these two hobbies would be a lifetime love and pursuit in the needlework industry.

Over the past 30 years in the needlework industry, I've served on the International Needlework Retailers Guild board as Secretary, and was founding President of a Sun Region Chapter of EGA serving four different times as President.

I've taught and attended many classes at needlework markets and specialize in conservation framing of needlework.

I restored a wedding dress (Whitework, Reticella, and Irish Crochet) for the National Trust Verdmont House in Bermuda and they awarded me a lifetime membership in the National Trust of Europe.

I have studied Silk Ribbon Embroidery in France, Reticella and Assisi Embroidery in Italy, Schwalm Embroidery in Germany, and together with Susan Greening Davis, co-sponsor needlework tours in Italy, England, Ireland, France, Germany, Belgium and many museum tours in Williamsburg, VA; Charleston, SC; Savannah, GA; and Greenfield Village in Dearborn, MI.

It has been a joy to capture the essence of Sibbel in our interpretation of her projects, which reflect and emphasize her lifestyle and joy in the simple treasures of life.

Lastly, I would like to thank my family for their love and support, and who have helped me to focus and live every needleworker's dream of owning a needlework shop.

Owner of Suwannee Valley Cross Stitch and Frame Shop in Trenton, Florida.

Thanks for thinking of me...Sally Criswell

Table of Contents

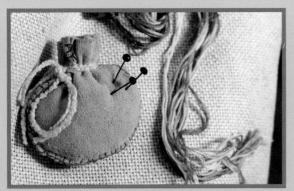

Introduction

Sibbel traveled into our lives a few years ago while we were hosting one of our "Heritage Needlework Tours" and exploring special places to study needlework history that we feel must not be forgotten. We were at our stop in Bruges, Belgium.

It was after breakfast and we had started out to view the lace museum and taste the chocolate!

A vintage sampler dealer had made an appointment to show her needlework samplers in a shop, and we were at the right place at the right time! We asked if we could be allowed to view and purchase one...or two!

There were many beautiful samplers but we knew the minute that Sibbel was shown, she must go home to America. Sally purchased her, and the next step was to go back to the hotel to unframe her to fit into a suitcase! Plus, we wanted to see the back of the needlework. The back of an embroidery piece can share many tales. The first was that Sibbel was not a very good embroiderer, even after she had studied. But, as many of us know, the back is not what counts. It is the front and what makes our hearts happy as we are stitching our pieces.

The dealer of the sampler shared as much history as was known. That served as the basis of *A Journey With Sibbel*, with additional extensive research on the meanings of the motifs for that era and region. The story that we present here is as true to what we could surmise for a young girl living in a charity house (orphanage) at this time in this region.

Sibbel has become our stitching sister and we have grown to love her more with each motif. Her original sampler has many motifs that we did not use. We selected the ones that told us the most about her journey.

We hope you enjoy this journey and join our sisterhood, too.

Still Stitching,
Susan Greening Davis and Sally Criswell

Sibbel's Show Piece:
Before You Begin

Materials

Fabric:
28 count Wichelt Linen / 14 count Aida
Natural Linen Brown (#76) / Natural Brown (#100)
  14" x 5"
Antique White (#101) / Antique White (#101) 22" x 5"
Sandstone (#21) / Desert Cream (#121) 20" x 5"
Vintage Blue Whisper (#3281-5139) / Vintage Blue
  Whisper (#3706-5139) 30" x 5"

Fiber:
The Gentle Art (DMC listed in parentheses):
  Brandy #0540 (422)
  Baked Clay #7088 (612)
  Flax #1150 (613)
  Buttermilk #7017 (677)
  Old Blue Paint #7006 (926)
  Woodrose #7018 (975)
  Highland Heather (778)
  DMC 3362
  DMC 3768
  DMC #12 Perle Coton, Ecru
  DMC #10 Cebelia Crochet Cotton, Ecru

Additional Materials:
Wooden spool or hanger
Lace no wider than ¾"
4 small wooden buttons
#7 Steel crochet hook

General Instructions

Pattern Information: All motifs are centered vertically. Each square on the chart equals 2 fabric threads, except where noted. Cross Stitches are over 2 fabric threads using 2 strands of floss, except where noted.
Each box on the Aida represents 2 threads on Linen.

Stitching Information

Do side finishing of edges before any other stitches.
Side stitching: Using 2 strands of The Gentle Art Old Blue Paint (DMC 926), do a Running Stitch down the long sides of the linen panels. Fold 1" back on each side. Count in 4 threads from the folded edge and stitch through both layers of fabric. Be sure all pieces match in width.

Stitches

All joining stitches use 1 strand #12 Perle Coton, except where noted.

Cross Stitch over 1 fabric thread, using 1 strand of floss
Cross Stitch over 2 fabric threads, using 2 strands of floss
Backstitch over 2 fabric threads, using 2 strands of floss
Running Stitch over 2 fabric threads, using 2 strands of floss
Vintage Hem Stitch
Tacking Stitch
Couching Stitch
Four-Sided "Box" Stitch
Feather Stitch
Herringbone Stitch
Blanket Stitch
Nun Stitch
Crochet

SIBBEL'S JOURNEY

I lived on a small Dutch farm until the age of 7. My younger sister, Inga, was 3 then. We were quiet but loved helping Papa outside with the chores and feeding the chickens with Mamma. There was wood to gather and clothes to be washed. We could help with bread-making and always were chosen to set the table. I was a very happy child.

During our last summer together, so many friends were stricken with the flux and died. Mamma and Papa joined our Savior then. The people from the small town we lived in were very kind, but everyone was poor and no one could take both of us. So, Inga went to live with our pastor and his wife, and I was sent to a charity house, an orphanage.

I was given a piece of one of Inga's shirts and a piece of my hem was cut off and given to Inga. This was done so maybe—someday—we could find each other again.

I had never been with so many children of all ages, and was very worried as to how we would all be taken care of at the orphanage. I soon learned that I was to do many things to take care of my needs there. The most important, and the one that I lacked the most skills in, was embroidery. I began my learning by stitching a marking sampler. This is a cross stitch of alphabets and numbers. This sampler would later be presented to people who brought their linens to the orphanage to be cleaned. We would mark the linens so we knew who they belonged to. The better your cross stitches, the more the people would pay. I was not very good yet, since I had never done this before. So, I did not get to mark anyone's linens to help earn my keep. We did not have a real teacher, just one of the guardians to show us how to make the marks.

Each of us was given a piece of wood that had some holes carved out of it. This is where we kept our threads so we would not lose them. My wood was called butternut. I liked the name of that tree!

I was glad when the marking sampler was completed. I would now get to make a show piece. This is what we unroll and lay on a table for patrons to look at before they choose one of us to come to work for them. But before I can start on the show piece, I have to stitch a weight.

Because the show piece will become longer and longer as pieces of fabric are sewn together, the weight will hold the fabric in place while I stitch on it. The pattern on the weight will be a tree. I have to draw my pattern from looking at another child's work. I try to do a good pattern since I will be using it over and over. After it is stitched, I will sew the fabric together and fill it with sawdust and sand. When my stitching weight is done, I will begin on my show piece.

My weight is done and now I will begin on my show piece samples. The show piece will have all kinds of pictures stitched on the fabric. The guardians tell me that these pictures all have different meanings. I will stitch the pictures, the guardians call them motifs, on small pieces of fabric and I will learn ways to join the fabric pieces together for finishing them off. This is an important part of each lesson. These pictures on the piece show what we can do for hire. My linen is hand woven and it is quite coarse. I am still not a very good stitcher.

The first picture I have to stitch for my sampler
is the tree I used on my stitching weight.

MOTIF PANEL NO. 1: SIBBEL 1735 AND TREE OF LIFE

Fabric: 7" x 5" piece of 28 count Wichelt Natural Brown Linen
(14 count Natural Brown Aida)

Fibers

Old Blue Paint (DMC 926) [•]
Flax (DMC 613) [x]
Baked Clay (DMC 612) [╱]
DMC 3768 [–]
Buttermilk (DMC 677) [+]

Instructions

Measure down 2" from the top of the fabric. Using 1 strand of floss,
Cross Stitch SIBBEL and date over 1 fabric thread. Leave 8 threads and
Cross Stitch the Tree of Life with 2 strands over 2 threads. Backstitch
the top two apples on the Tree using Old Blue Paint (DMC 926).
Backstitch the remaining apples on Tree using Buttermilk (DMC 677).

Joining Instructions

Top Joining: Using the 2" at the top, fold the fabric back and
attach a wooden spool or other hanger.

Bottom Joining: Many times, fabric would run out and a
young stitcher would be taught a technique to join pieces.
Our first joining lesson is the Vintage Hem Stitch. From the
base of the Tree, count down 6 threads. Cut the horizontal
thread in the middle of the fabric. Carefully unweave it until
you get to the side folds. To do the first fold, count down 18
threads from the withdrawn thread area and fold to the back.
Fold this piece straight. Then tuck the raw edge of the fabric
inside of the fold flap. Be sure it sets so the naked thread
gusset is visible. Hem Stitch using 1 strand of #12 Perle Coton.

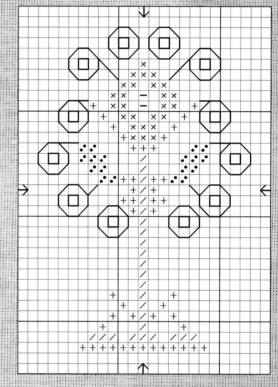

Design size: 21W x 31H

*The Tree of Life, with golden apples,
represents immortality. It also symbolizes
knowledge and good.*

Design size: 72W x 8H

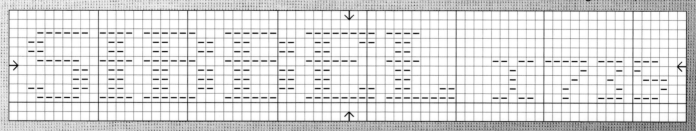

Now that I have completed my tree, I am learning to hem the edge. I will do this for the first two pieces of fabric that will be joined together. I have been told that this is the most important edge for a girl to know. Table linens, bed coverings, wall hangings, it seems almost everything is completed with this stitch.

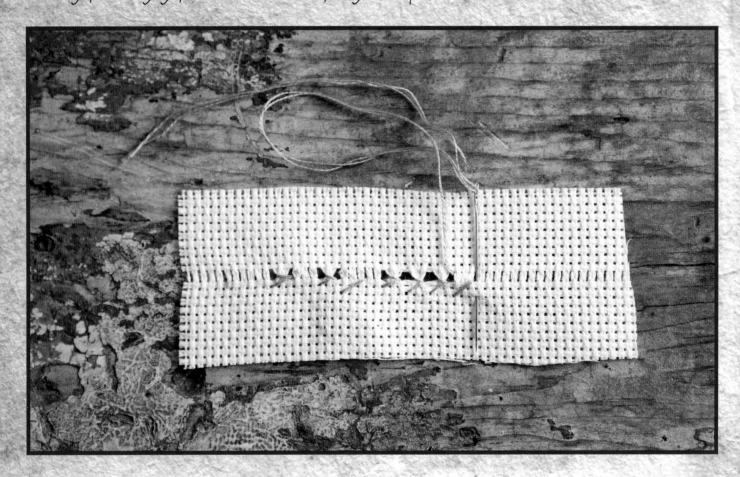

First I must cut a thread on my linen. It is cut in the middle of a side, top or bottom—or all four sides. Then I must carefully unpick this thread to the edge until it meets other threads I have unpicked. I need to be patient as this thread is saved and used for the stitching. I do not want it to break because shorter lengths are hard to work with. Next, my teacher shows me how to make folded edges. This is done with a smooth stone that has been heated on the fire, and a bit of wet cloth. I must be very careful not to ruin the fabric with the hot stone. I am frightened of the fire and the stone. It is easy to get burned by placing the stone on the fire or

when it must be removed with a good sturdy tree branch. To pick it up, the stone must be wrapped with another cloth. I have to be very careful. A straight fold is done for the outsides of the cloth, folding them to the back of the linen. I make sure it is even, for when the heated stone is placed on the wet cloth, it keeps the folds in place. Then I must do another fold. This fold sets below the place where I took away the thread. When all is done, I will do the hemming. I must make sure it is even. My teacher says that I will need to do it again on a second piece of linen. I will get better, and then she will teach me how to connect two small pieces of linen together.

The next two patterns to be cross stitched are pictures of a windmill and a tiny bird with a tail pointing down.

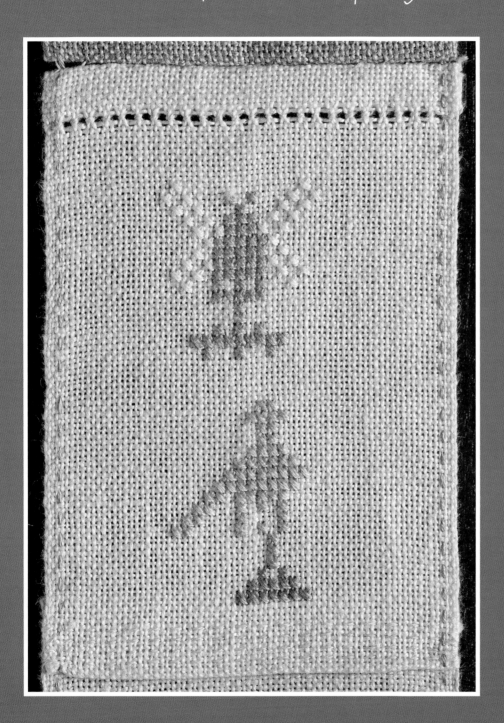

The windmill reminds me of my farm home. We would watch the windmills go around and around. They would grind the corn and wheat for us. I wonder what Inga is doing. After my stitching time, I will go to the kitchen and wash dishes. More children have arrived and we are sleeping four in a bed. The mattress is straw, and itchy, but we are warmer now.

MOTIF PANEL NO. 2: WINDMILL AND BIRD

Fabric: 6" x 5" piece of 28 count Wichelt Vintage Blue Whisper Linen (14 count Vintage Blue Whisper Aida)

Fibers
Brandy (DMC 422) [✓]
Baked Clay (DMC 612) [□]
Buttermilk (DMC 677) [+]
Old Blue Paint (DMC 926) [∴]

Instructions
Measure down 1 ¾" from the top of the fabric. Cross Stitch the Windmill.
Leave 8 threads and Cross Stitch the Bird

Joining Instructions
Top Joining: Count up 11 threads from the top of the Windmill. Cut the 12th horizontal thread in the middle of the fabric. Carefully unweave it until you get to the side folds. A good habit is to unweave the threads on the backside of the fabric. Then the tails are ready to place in the fold for the hem.

Do the first fold 10 threads above the withdrawn gusset. Make sure to fold this straight. Tuck the raw edge of the fabric inside of the fold flap. Be sure it sets so the naked thread gusset is visible. Hem Stitch using 1 strand of Perle Coton. Tack the two Hem Stitched edges together with 1 strand of Perle Coton.

Bottom Joining: To join the bottom of the fabric, count down 13 threads from the bottom of the Bird. Fold the excess fabric to the front. This will set inside, or "cuff," into the top fold of the next fabric piece.

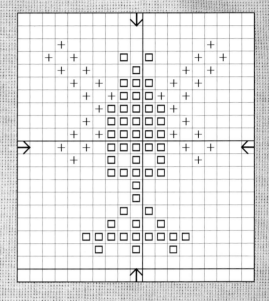

Design size: 15W x 17H
Sibbel's windmill was called a post windmill and it would have been used to grind corn.

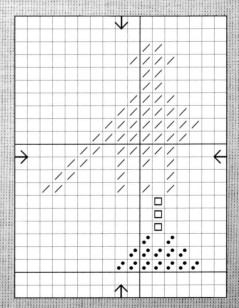

Design size: 13W x 18H
Birds are considered spirits in the air and were a symbol for peace.

The next two patterns to stitch are of a sailing ship and a tree that looks like a flower.

I had seen sailing ships with Mamma and Papa before I moved here. We went to the seashore and watched the ships coming into the harbor. It was a beautiful sight. Papa said they were bringing supplies for our town and the people who lived in our area. Stitching the ship's sail was hard. It has two long stitches that were not supposed to be pulled tight or left loose. I did tiny stitches on top of the long stitches to keep them in place. The tree that looks like a flower reminds me of Mamma's flower garden. Inga and I would pull weeds and water the garden for her. We do not have flowers here, except for when the potato plants bloom, or sometimes when one of the children dies and a clergyman puts a flower on their grave.

I have also learned to cross stitch a crown and a basket. There are many different kinds of crowns, each one telling us the importance of the crown's owner. We embroider these crowns on linens for people. When families bring their laundry to us, the specific crown tells us what linens belong to which family. I want to mark the linens of someone who has a special crown. That way I will make more money to help the orphanage pay for me and some of my friends for the food and things we need.

The basket was fun to do and makes me hope that I will have something to keep my stitching supplies in someday. Now I just put them in a neat pile by the side of the wall where my bed is. This is not very good in the winter because the snow blows in through the cracks in the walls and then our supplies can be ruined, especially the needles! Sometimes rats start chewing the fabric too.

MOTIF PANEL NO. 3: SAILING SHIP, CARNATION, CROWN AND BASKET

Fabric: 9" x 5" piece of 28 count Wichelt Sandstone Linen (14 count Desert Cream Aida)

Fibers
Brandy (DMC 422) [∕]
Baked Clay (DMC 612) [▯]
Flax (DMC 613) [x]
Buttermilk (DMC 677) [+]
Old Blue Paint (DMC 926) [∙∙]
DMC 3768 [–]

Instructions
Measure down 1 ¼" from the top of the fabric. Cross Stitch the Sailing Ship. Backstitch the sails using Baked Clay (DMC 612). Tack down the Backstitch where shown.
Leave 8 threads and Cross Stitch the Carnation.
Leave 8 threads and Cross Stitch the Crown.
Leave 8 threads and Cross Stitch the Basket.

Joining Instructions
Top Joining: To join the top with Motif No. 2, count 13 threads up from the top of the Sailing Ship and fold fabric to the back. Set the blue fabric from Motif No. 2 inside this fold, like a "cuff." Do a Running Stitch with #12 Perle Coton. Begin with a knot hidden in the crease of the folds on the pieces. Bring the needle straight up by a vertical thread through all layers of fabric. Begin 5 threads up from the fold and do the next to the bottom row of stitching first. Keep the fabric lined up perfectly and go back and forth, through all layers. Each beginning and ending stitch is worked around the outside edge of the fabric twice. Then stitch 2 rows, so the stitches match up, above this row and 1 row below this row. There are 2 threads between these rows of Running Stitches. When you get to the end, do a small sewing knot on the backside.

Bottom Joining: Fold 1 inch of fabric to front of needlework.

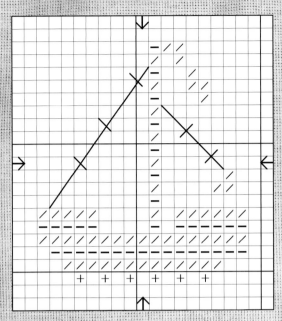

Design size: 17W x 19H

Sailing ships represented freedom and hope.

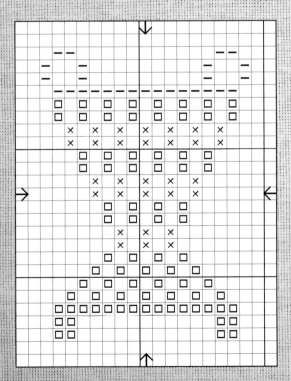

Design size: 17W x 23H

Baskets had utilitarian uses with women. They were used to gather laundry, food, flowers, or personal treasures.

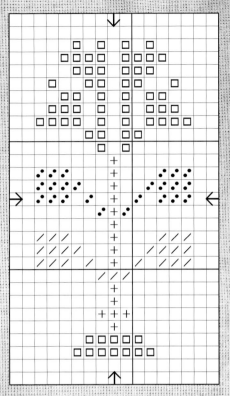

Design size: 13W x 25H

A carnation also would have been known by the name Gilly Flower. They were equated to true love (red carnations) and poverty.

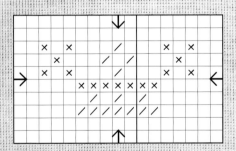

Design size: 13W x 6H

Crowns were one of the most common motifs in samplers. The symbolisms of eternity or the crown of life would have been explanations for their popularity.

There's only a little bit of fabric left, so I have to add a new piece to it. We do this by folding and stitching the pieces together. The folding was easier than the hem stitch, but I was careful not to lose any of the threads that were left since I do not have very much fabric.

Besides my new fabric, I was given a small piece of hide, some sand from the seashore, and a string. I have put the sand into the hide and tied the ends of the hide together as tight as I could. When my needle gets dull, I add water to the sand in my pouch and spin the needle to keep it smooth and help with the burrs. My stitching must be getting better to have been given these materials. I wish they could help with the eye of my needle, as it is starting to break and I have to work carefully to keep it together.

My next little piece of linen has another carnation and crown. Both of these are different patterns than what I have already stitched. It is good to do different patterns!

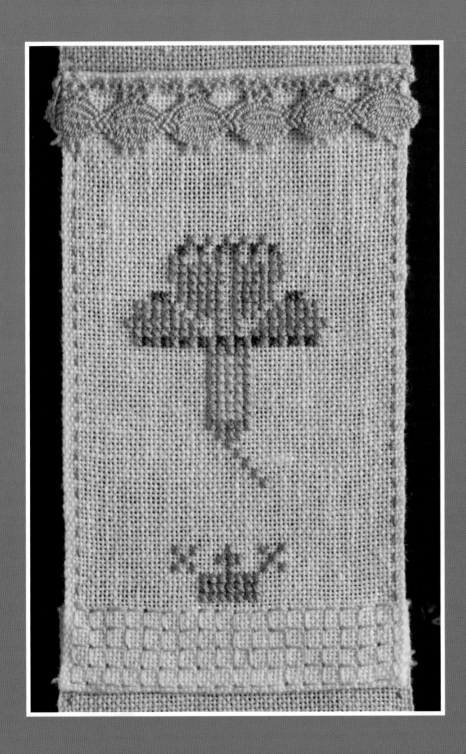

MOTIF PANEL NO. 4: GILLY FLOWER AND CROWN

Fabric: 7" x 5" piece 28 count Wichelt Antique White Linen (14 count Antique White Aida)

Fibers
Brandy (DMC 422) [✓]
Baked Clay (DMC 612) [□]
Flax (DMC 613) [x]
DMC 3768 [–]

Instructions
Measure down 2 ¼". Cross Stitch Gilly Flower.
Leave 12 fabric threads and Cross Stitch the Crown.

Joining Instructions
Top Joining: Fold 1" of fabric to the back. Cuff this inside the Sandstone fabric from Motif Panel No. 3. Place lace on top of the folds and attach using a Tacking Stitch.

Bottom Joining: Leave 16 fabric threads beneath the Crown and fold excess fabric to the back.

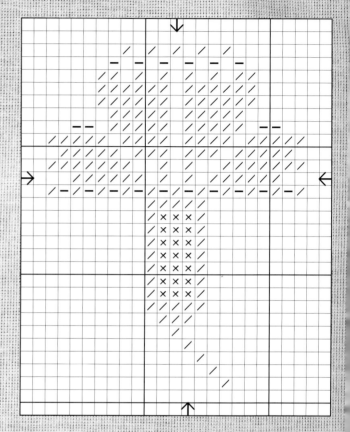

Design size: 21W x 27H
Many times, the Gilly Flower was used to symbolize the Holy Trinity.

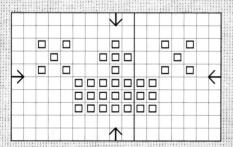

Design size: 13W x 6H
Different types of crowns defined ranks of noble men. The crowns would have been stitched to mark linens to identify a family's rank.

The flower was much easier to stitch. I believe I did better too, because the guardian did not ask me to take any of my stitches out.

Last week, we were taken into town to visit a clergyman to hear his sermon. I was surprised to see that we were the only children wearing the type of clothes we had on. Our clothes are all the same two colors, red and black. The front is black and the back is red. Other children had on all different colors and kinds of pants, skirts, and jackets. When I asked the guardian about this, she told me that we all dressed the same so the people of the town knew where we lived and would help us back if we got lost. I do not know how that would happen because we have to stay in our rows and hold hands.

The hide and the sand I was given have really helped. My needle slides through the fabric better now, and this helps me do nicer stitches. I am working very hard to keep the needle from breaking any more than it is. It is not as strong as some of the other children's, and the eye is starting to split. My work is not good enough yet for a new one. Sometimes when a child passes on, their needle is given to a good stitcher—even boys! Needles are very important in our home. We could not learn to earn our keep with our stitching if we did not have them.

A teacher has come to the orphanage! Miss Lena is from Italy and looks like she has been in the sun. She has dark hair and eyes, while most of us have very light colored hair and blue eyes. The boys are first to learn, but some of the girls will learn to read and do sums. I think I would like this. If I complete my chores quickly, I will have time to sit in these lessons.

I am sure that I must be improving with my embroidery. First, the guardians gave me fabric to make a pouch for storage, and now Miss Lena has given me a very small piece of something called lace from Italy. It is so beautiful! She explained that it is all made by hand and that some of us may learn to do this one day.

We are going to add another piece of fabric to the one we have been stitching on and put this lace onto where the two linen pieces join. First, I must fold one of the edges. Then, I lay the new piece of fabric on top of my old one. My stitches must be very small and even. There is just enough lace to fold to the back, so it sets correctly on the front. I still have some threads left from the older piece of fabric, and they are the same color as the lace, so I will use this to sew on the

lace. The guardian says it must be sewn on so the stitches do not show, but the linen fabric does show through the holes in the lace. The knots for starting and stopping have to be very small and not show. I have not been very good at making these small knots. But this time, I will be better.

This is another important lesson. The women who will have me sew for them will have lots of lace, and they like it sewn onto their petticoats and pin cushions. I cannot imagine that. My petticoat is very coarse and plain.

A new girl named Jytte has come to the orphanage, and she knows how to do stitching. She has some pretty threads and she is giving me a piece of a pretty rose color. I am going to use it on the trunk of a tree. She has a very good needle. I am waiting to get better so I can have one. The eye on my needle is wearing and I have to work to keep it together and keep the threads smooth. Jytte let me stitch my tree trunk with her needle and the pretty thread. The needle made stitching better, but I ran out of the pretty thread, so I did not finish my tree.

This stitched motif of the Unfinished Tree is from the original sampler.

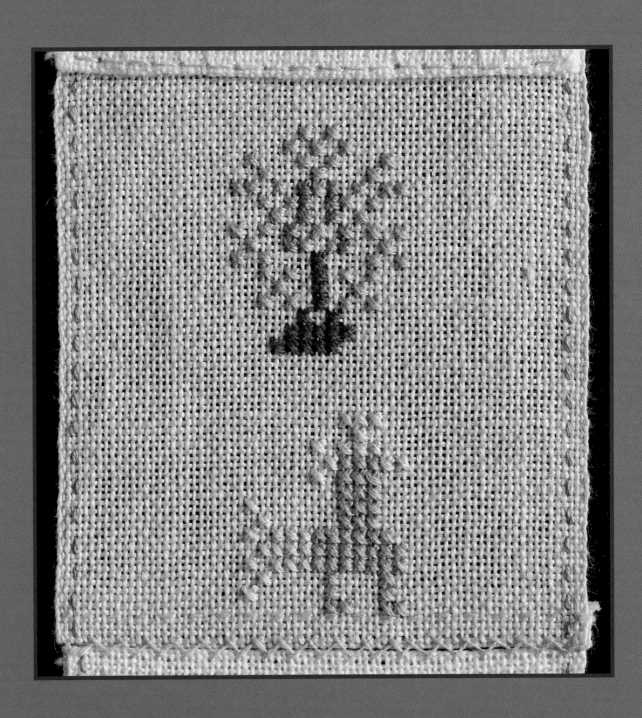

MOTIF PANEL NO. 5: UNFINISHED TREE AND BIRD (PEACOCK)

Fabric: 9" x 5" piece of 28 count Wichelt Vintage Blue Whisper Linen (14 count Vintage Blue Whisper Aida)

Fibers
Brandy (DMC 422) [/]
Flax (DMC 613) [x]
Old Blue Paint (DMC 926) [··]
Woodrose (DMC 975) [♥]

Instructions
Measure down 1 ½". Cross Stitch the Tree.
Leave 8 fabric threads and Cross Stitch the Bird.

Joining Instructions
Top Joining: Fold 1" to the front of the fabric. Cuff the fabric to the Motif No. 4 piece of fabric. Do a Four-Sided Stitch (called the "Box" Stitch during Sibbel's time) across the fabric using one strand of #12 Perle Coton. Do a total of 4 rows. Do not "double stitch" where the stitches touch each other.

Bottom Joining: Fold 1" of fabric to the back.

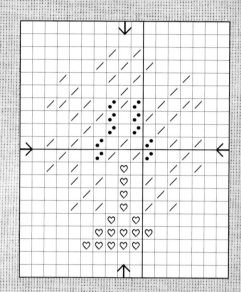

Design size: 13W x 16H

In this motif, we see a little section of new color being used. As the special thread ran out in Sibbel's time, motifs would often remain unfinished, like this tree. This type of cone tree was very popular during this era. Many were used as "fillers" in spot motif samplers.

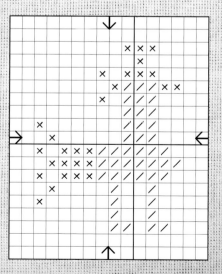

Design size: 12W x 15H
Vanity and pride were associated with this bird.

I am hoping that Jytte will be my friend. It's not easy to have a special friend here. There are so many children here, but we all are busy working and sometimes children even get to go home with a new family. I wonder what Inga is doing now. She would be getting taller, as I am.

I am learning a new stitch to put my two pieces of fabric together. It is called the Box Stitch. I will be folding the two edges inside of each other so my back looks better. My guardian says I am doing better in my stitching. This is good!

I am back to work cross stitching. Next, I am to do a tree with tulips. It reminds me of my home. I have not seen tulips in a long time. We had so many colors in

Photo courtesy of Sander Klaver (freeimages.com/photo/1443439)

our garden. Inga and I picked them one time—every one of them—and gave them to Mamma. She was not happy, but we saw the twinkle in her eye. We did not do that again. She told us that they would stay prettier a lot longer if we left them alone. She was right because they didn't last very long in a jar of water.

Below my tulip tree, I am going to cross stitch a heart. Mary, another girl here, says that is a motif that many people use when they are in love or getting married.

I came to the orphanage when I was 7 years old. I know that we have had two winters so I must be 9. I now get to help some of the younger girls learn how to thread their needles and tie a knot at the end of their thread. I remember that it took a lot of practice for me to learn to do this, so I am trying to be patient. Their little fingers are fast but they have trouble holding onto their needles. These needles are pieces of bone or a fish spine where an eye has been carved into the end. It is what I started with, too.

I have also been given a wooden bobbin to wind my show piece on. I folded a small hem on the raw edge of the fabric, and then tacked it around the wooden bobbin so the stitches did not show.

When someone comes to have us do needlework for them, we lay the show pieces on a table for display. The patrons look over the show pieces and then choose who they want to embroider for them. I am now part of the group that is chosen from!

Today, I started my stitching by doing a tree with birds and grapes. I have never seen or tasted a grape. I wonder what it tastes like. I am going to ask Miss Lena since she is from Italy. The guardian says they have lots of grapes there, and that they make wine there. The people from Italy drink wine with all of their meals. The only wine I know about is in church.

MOTIF PANEL NO. 6: TREE WITH TULIPS, WINGED HEART, BIRDS WITH GRAPES

Fabric: 9" x 5" piece of 28 count Wichelt Antique White Linen (14 count Antique White Aida)

Fibers

Brandy (DMC 422) [∕]
Baked Clay (DMC 612) [□]
Flax (DMC 613) [x]
Buttermilk (DMC 677) [+]
Old Blue Paint (DMC 926) [∴]
Woodrose (DMC 975) [♡]
DMC 3768 [–]

Instructions

Measure down 1 ¾". Cross Stitch the Tree with Tulips.
Leave 10 threads and Cross Stitch the Winged Heart.
Leave 10 threads and Cross Stitch the Birds with Grapes.

Joining Instructions

Top Joining: Fold 1" of fabric to the front. Make sure the fabric is folded evenly. Cuff the fabric pieces together. Using 1 strand of #12 Perle Coton, do a Herringbone Stitch through all layers of fabric. Work stitch so it covers 2 threads below the join fold and 2 threads above the join fold. Count up 3 threads above the Herringbone and do a Running Stitch. Count down 2 threads below the Herringbone and Cross Stitch so that they match the "mountain" points of the Herringbone.

Bottom Joining: Fold 1" of fabric to the front.

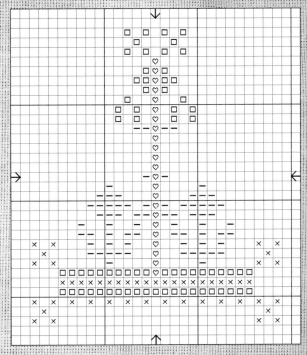

Design size: 27W x 31H
A tree with tulips is indicative of the Netherlands. It symbolizes perfect love.

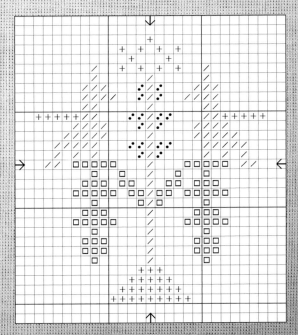

Design size: 25W x 28H
This is a combination motif. Grapes represented the Blood of Christ. A pair of birds was attributed to eternal life.

Design size: 19W x 10H
A winged heart symbolizes prayer.

It is my turn to learn a new stitch to put two more pieces of linen together. This one looks very different. It looks like the bones of a herring fish. I have seen them when those fish are cleaned.

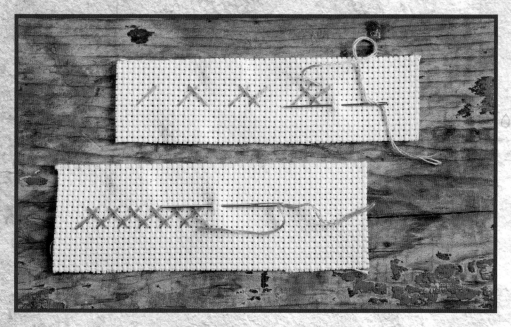

I am going to do the fold on the edges of the fabrics. I have not had to do this for a while; I do not like this part of stitching. I am told that this time it has to be the best ever.

I learned many things today. The threads on the fabric are not the same sizes, and they are tighter together at the sides. This makes my stitches different looking. It is because of the weaving. I have a very small loom that my Papa made for me. He whittled it out of twigs. I got to bring it with me and I have made some potholders.

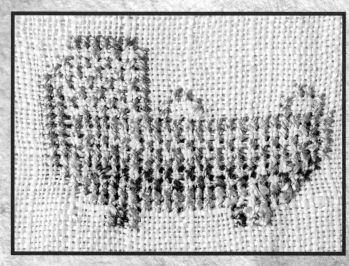

This stitched motif of the Baby Basket is from the original sampler.

It is time to learn some new things. I am learning to crochet! This is the prettiest stitching, ever. It looks just like lace. I like that I have learned to do this on the sides of my fabric. On this piece of fabric, I am stitching a baby basket and a dog. There are no dogs or cats here. Papa would not let us have any either, unless a stray cat hid in our barn and ate the mice. Inga and I did not like the mice in our beds. (It happens here all the time in the cold weather.)

MOTIF PANEL NO. 7: BABY BASKET AND DOG

Fabric: 5" x 5" piece of 28 count Wichelt Vintage Blue
Whisper Linen (14 count Vintage Blue Whisper Aida)

Fibers
Brandy (DMC 422) [/]
Baked Clay (DMC 612) [□]
Flax (DMC 613) [x]
DMC 3768 [–]

Instructions
Measure down 1 1/4". Cross Stitch the Baby Basket.
Leave 4 threads and Cross Stitch the Dog.

Finishing Instructions
Crochet around edge or add lace.

SIBBEL'S CROCHET EDGE *Created by Sally Criswell*

DMC #10 Cebelia Crochet Cotton, Ecru
Size #7 Steel Crochet Hook

Abbreviations:
CH=Chain Stitch; SC=Single Crochet; DC=Double Crochet; SS=Slip Stitch.

Count up 14 threads from top and bottom of stitched design. Pull 15th
thread completely out. On each side count out 20 threads, beyond
stitching, and withdraw the 21st thread. This will give you precise folding
lines to fold fabric back to begin your crochet edging.

Row 1: Attach the thread in the middle of the top row (front side facing
you) and SC around the square stitching through both layers. When you get
to a corner, put 3 SC in corner stitch and continue to SC along the side until
you get to the next corner, put 3 SC in corner stitch and continue around
until you get back to the beginning stitch and SS to top of first SC to join.

Row 2: CH 4, skip 2 SC and SS into next SC. Repeat all the way around
the square ending up with 10 CH 4 loops on each side all the way
around. (40 loops) Join at base of first loop.

Row 3: In each loop, (SC, DC, SC) all the way around. Join at base with
a SS. Leave a 4 inch tail of thread, which you will thread up and run
through the back stitches to hide and cut off. Trim away excess fabric on
the back side where it is folded.

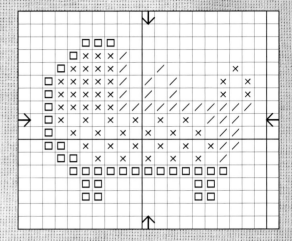

Design size: 17W X 13H
*A baby basket symbolized maternal love
and was considered a household item.*

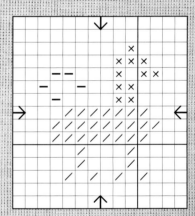

Design size: 10W X 11H
*Dogs were often considered
watch dogs to chase away
the Devil. When the motif is
paired with the baby basket,
it is especially symbolic of
protection.*

The guardian says I'll be learning lots of new things this year. The crocheting is the first. I have also been working on sewing tucks and hole openings for clothing.

It is March and soon spring will be here. That means there will be wild berries, and that is the best!

MOTIF PANEL NO. 8: TREE WITH CONEFLOWERS

Fabric: 5" x 5" piece 28 count Wichelt Sandstone Linen
(14 count Desert Cream Aida)

Fibers
Baked Clay (DMC 612) [□]
DMC 3768 [–]

Instructions
Measure down 1 ½". Cross Stitch Tree with Coneflowers.

Joining Instructions
Top Joining: Fold 1" of fabric to back and cuff fabric pieces.
Set crochet, or lace, on the fold and do a Tacking Stitch.

Bottom Joining: Fold 1" of fabric to the back of the
stitching.

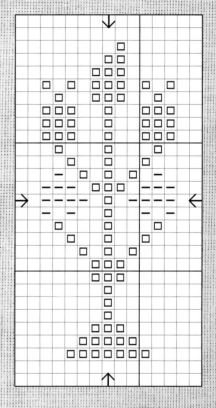

Design size: 11W x 25H
Tree with Coneflowers, or a fruit-bearing tree, often meant the Resurrection. The number of fruit could also signify the number of children in a family.

My work has gotten much better throughout the year, and I have learned many ways to join linen for when I run out. We only get small pieces of linen here since the fabric costs a lot of money. The bigger pieces are saved for work to be done for pay. Sometimes people from the village bring us leftover fabric and the linen isn't the same color most of the time. If someone dies, we sometimes get their unfinished work. That is sad for me to do.

My roll of stitching is getting longer and this is good. It is almost as long as I am tall! When a patron comes to look at our work, mine is now studied. No one has chosen me to embroider for them yet, but I am hopeful.

It's summer now, and one thing I like about summer are the nights and all of the pretty fireflies. We tried to catch them one night, but you never know where they are going to be! I would like to be a firefly, so beautiful and free to go anywhere you want to. I hope to find Inga someday; we can be like the pretty fireflies and fly away together.

Jytte has taught me to be a slower stitcher and to watch my work. There's been talk of Jytte leaving to live with a family to do all of their mending and stitching. We all know this is what happens here, but she has been my special friend. I hope they don't take her away.

I just stitched a man and a woman. They look like they are holding hands. I will use them for weddings. Many of the pictures I am stitching will be important for families to have done.

MOTIF PANEL NO. 9: MAN AND WOMAN AND AUTUMN TREE

Fabric: 6" x 5" piece of 28 count Wichelt Antique White (14 count Antique White Aida)

Fibers

Brandy (DMC 422) [/]
Baked Clay (DMC 612) [□]
Flax (DMC 613) [x]
Old Blue Paint (DMC 926) [∴]
DMC 3768 [–]

Instructions

Measure down 1 ½". Cross Stitch the Man and Woman. Leave 8 fabric threads and Cross Stitch the Autumn Tree. Backstitch Man's hair with Baked Clay.

Joining Instructions

Top Joining: Fold 1" to the front of the fabric. Cuff the fabric to the Motif No. 8 piece of fabric. Do a Four-Sided Stitch (called the "Box" Stitch during Sibbel's time) across the fabric using one strand of #12 Perle Coton. Do a total of 4 rows. Do not "double stitch" where the stitches touch each other.

Bottom Joining: Fold 1" of fabric to the back.

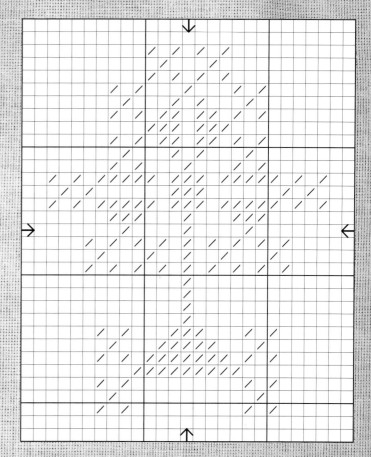

Design size: 23W x 29H

The Autumn Tree is a motif referring to the season.

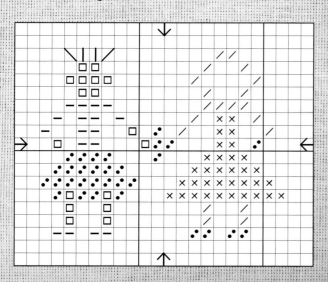

Design size: 20W x 15H

These images are from the family category of sampler motifs. The holding of hands represented marriage.

More children are arriving. Something called the Black Death has happened and many people are dying. The head matron writes as much information down in a book as she knows about the new child. Sometimes children are just left by our entrance gate; other times, folks from the town bring in children who have been left to wander the streets, alone. I see many scraps of fabric left with the head matron, too.

I am helping with the new children. When they arrive, we wash them and scrub their heads for lice, cut their hair, burn their old clothes and give them different clothing to wear. It seems like a long time ago since they did this to me. With more children to feed, we are sharing kettles of food. The girls eat in one area and the boys in another. Four girls eat from the same kettle, while someone reads the Bible.

I have stitched another flower. It's similar to the carnation, and is called a Gilly Flower. I am also learning harder stitches to keep my fabric pieces together. I have learned so much here. I am lucky to be in this home. I have learned that most homes are not as good at teaching children how to do all the things we have learned here. The governors who are in charge of us are shop keepers and many of the boys will go to work for them when they are old enough.

MOTIF PANEL NO. 10: GILLY FLOWER WITH BERRIES

Fabric: 4 ½" x 5" piece of 28 count Wichelt Vintage Blue Whisper Linen (14 count Vintage Blue Whisper Aida)

Fibers
Brandy (DMC 422) [/]
Flax (DMC 613) [x]
DMC 3768 [–]

Instructions
Measure down 1 ¾". Cross Stitch the Gilly Flower.

Joining Instructions
Top Joining: Fold 1" of fabric to the front and cuff with the fabric from Motif Panel No. 9. Cross Stitch through all layers with DMC 3768. Attach a small wooden button on each end.

Bottom Joining: Fold 1" of fabric to the back.

Design size: 27W x 20H

According to Christian religion, the Gilly Flower made its first appearance when Mary's tears fell to the ground on her way to Calvary. Fruit on the flowers indicated a celebration in life.

Jytte has started working outside the orphanage. When she leaves the orphanage, she must carry a coin and give it to the head of the house she is working at. That tells them she is allowed to leave the orphanage and work that day. Every night, she comes back and tells me of her day. She has told me of the nice house she goes to. I am happy for her, but I miss her.

I have come to love to do my stitching. After the Gilly Flower, I stitched a peacock and a flower pot. I have learned to put my small pieces of fabric together with some wooden buttons we were given. I know that they belonged on one of the pieces of clothing that someone used to wear. I believe they must have died, since that is the only reason we would have gotten them. The guardians cut them off shirts when they cannot be fixed anymore. It is important to do different stitching things, but it is hard to know that someone has died for us to get buttons.

MOTIF PANEL NO. 11: PEACOCK AND FLOWER POT

Fabric: 6" x 5" piece 28 count Wichelt Sandstone Linen
(14 count Desert Cream Aida)

Fibers

Baked Clay (DMC 612) [□]
Old Blue Paint (DMC 926) [∵]
DMC 3768 [–]

Instructions

Measure down 1 ½". Cross Stitch the Peacock.
Leave 6 threads and Cross Stitch the Flower Pot.
Backstitch peacock with Baked Clay.

Joining Instructions

Top Joining: Fold 1" of fabric to the front. Cuff this piece with
the fabric from Motif No. 10. Cross Stitch through all layers
with DMC 3768. Attach a small wooden button on each end.

Bottom Joining: Fold 1" of fabric to the back.

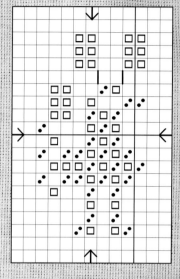

Design size: 9W x 16H

*Peacocks stood for luxury
and kingly demeanor.*

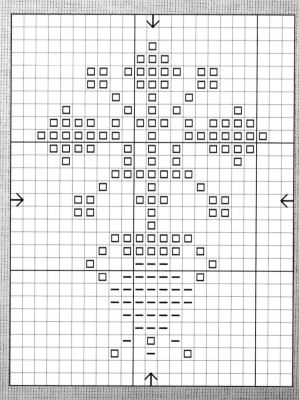

Design size: 19W x 25H

*The flower pot was
associated with Scripture.
An earthenware pot
symbolized the Virgin's
lowly birth. A glass pot
symbolized the purity of
the Holy Virgin.*

I know that my time is coming to go out and work in a household. I have been here for seven years. I am 14. It seems like such a long time since I lived with my own family. I hope that when I do leave, my new home will be kind.

I just finished stitching another tree! I think we stitch so many plants and trees because they are growing everywhere here. We did not have that many on our farm. The motif I am doing now is of a linen cupboard. It's every girl's hope to have one of these. Mamma did have one started for me, but Inga got to take it with her when she was taken by the pastor and his wife. I guess they thought that she would have a better chance to get married than I did. I remember all of the pretty things that were in the cupboard. Mamma had embroidered pillowcases, sheets and wall hangings. She had even put in some of her own from her linen chest.

MOTIF PANEL NO. 12: TREE AND LINEN CHEST

Fabric: 7" x 5" piece 28 count Wichelt Antique White Linen (14 count Antique White Aida)

Fibers
Baked Clay (DMC 612) [□]
Old Blue Paint (DMC 926) [∴]
DMC 3768 [–]

Instructions
Measure down 1 ½". Cross Stitch the Tree.
Leave 8 fabric threads and Cross Stitch the Linen Chest.

Joining Instructions
Top Joining: Fold 1" of fabric to the front. Cuff fabric edges. Do a Running Stitch using 2 strands of Woodrose (DMC 975) through all layers of fabric.

Bottom Joining: Fold 1" of fabric to the back.

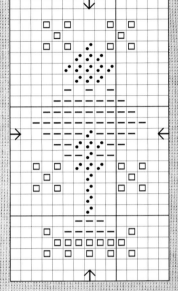

Design size: 11W x 22H

Trees are one of the most common motifs in samplers. Sibbel must have enjoyed stitching them, as her sampler included so many!

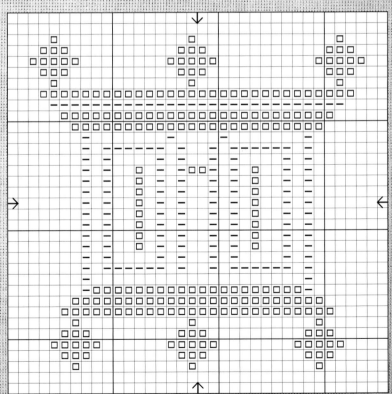

Design size: 32W x 31H

A "kas," as a linen chest was called in samplers from the Netherlands, could be identified by the double doors and the bun feet. It was a great source of pride for any housewife to be able to store linens here.

There is no time to stitch anything for ourselves here. We must always be busy doing some kind of work, or stitching on our show piece. Mine is very long now. I always roll it up very carefully and place it in my little bag.

A man and woman have come to see my stitching and look at me. That means that they may want me to work for them and maybe live with them! They did not speak to me, only to the guardian, but they seemed nice. They looked me up and down and checked my stitching. They have 11 children and need someone to mend and repair things for the children and in the house.

MOTIF PANEL NO. 13: BIRD WITH FLOWERS

Fabric: 5" x 5" piece of 28 count Wichelt Vintage Blue Whisper Linen (14 count Vintage Blue Whisper Aida)

Fibers

Brandy (DMC 422) [╱]
Flax (DMC 613) [x]
Woodrose (DMC 975) [♥]
DMC 3768 [–]

Instructions

Measure down 1 ½". Cross Stitch the Bird with Flowers.

Joining Instructions

Top Joining: Fold 1" of fabric to the front and cuff with fabric from Motif Panel No. 12. Secure a piece of lace on top of cuff with a Tacking Stitch.

Bottom Joining: Fold 1" of fabric to the back.

Design size: 27W x 30H

The bird with flowers symbolized happiness and beauty in nature.

It has happened! I am out working. I am living in a home with the family who visited the orphanage to look at my work. It has been an exciting time. The mistress wanted me to stitch a weight for her. She had some lace that belonged to her grandmother. I put it around the edge of the weight and I found the rest of my wooden buttons and the shell lace that Miss Lena gave me. I put them on the weight and my mistress liked it.

Then I was given some wool that had been a scarf that belonged to one of the boys. He had ripped it badly. Wool is good for needles and keeping them from rusting. I made a needle book for one of the daughters and used this wool.

I did such a good job on the needle book that I was asked to make a small sewing kit for the oldest daughter. This wool was from one of her father's coats. I got to keep a small piece of this wool to finish my own pocket purse. I needed a pretty one to show the importance of where I work. I am sad that I have to wear it under my skirt or apron as it is so pretty. But it makes me feel special to have this.

My life has changed very much over the past years. What I have learned, with my needle, is very important. Even though it is work, it has given me great joy.

Still Stitching, Sibbel

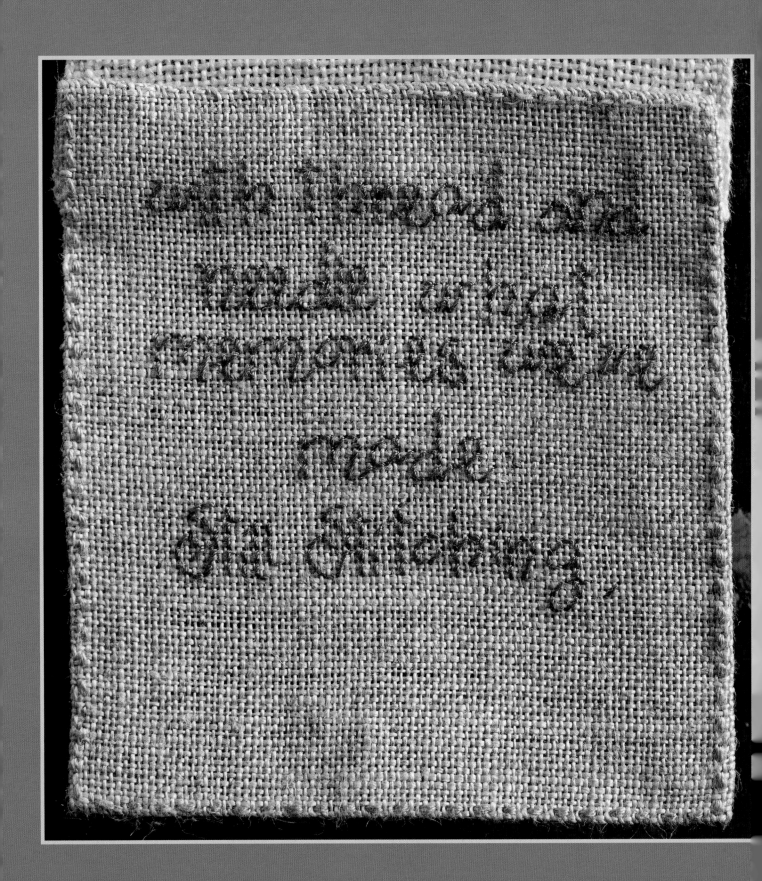

MOTIF PANEL NO. 14: VERSE

Fabric: 5" x 5" piece 28 count Wichelt Natural Brown Linen (14 count Natural Brown Aida)

Instructions
Backstitch verse using 2 strands of DMC 3768 floss. Personalize underneath Still Stitching with the alphabet provided on page 69.

Joining Instructions
Top Joining: Fold 1" fabric to the back. Do a Running Stitch using #12 Perle Coton.
Bottom Joining: Fold 1" of fabric to the back.

Finishing Instructions
Turn the bottom of the linen to the back side and continue to do a Running Stitch with DMC 3768.

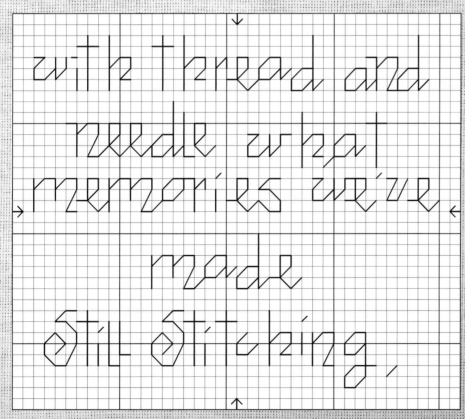

Design size: 38W x 32H

PROJECTS

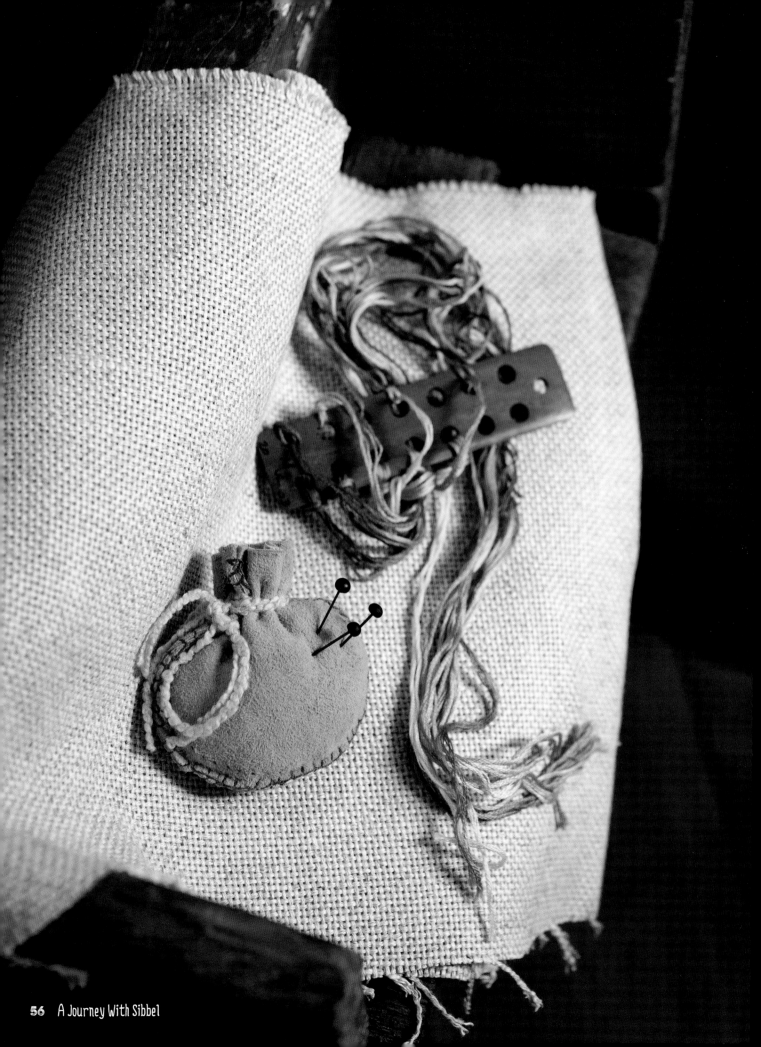

LEATHER PIN CUSHION

Materials

Two pieces of 5" x 5" pieces of leather (or wool or fabric)
Sand (aquarium sand), wool batting, or emery

Fiber

Woodrose (DMC 975)

Stitches

Blanket Stitch

Instructions

Using the template provided, cut 2 pieces of leather.
Using the Blanket Stitch, join the 2 pieces together using
a very sharp needle with 2 strands of floss.

Fill the pin cushion with sand. If you are using leather,
you can close the top by tying it with string once filled.
If you are using wool or fabric, you may want to stitch
the top edge closed.

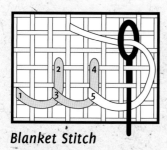

Blanket Stitch

Leather Pin Cushion

This pouch would have been used by Sibbel to keep her sewing supplies in, including her sewing roll, crochet hooks, needles, buttons, scissors, and threads.

Materials
Burlap: 2 pieces measuring 8" x 10" each
Cord or Twine

Fiber
Woodrose (DMC 975)

Stitches
Feather Stitch

Instructions
Cut 2 pieces of burlap 8" x 10".
Feather Stitch the 2 pieces of burlap together using 3 strands of Woodrose (DMC 975). Measure down 1" from the top edge of the burlap and weave a cord or twine along the top at random intervals to make the drawstring. Tie a bow and fill with your treasures.

The **Feather Stitch** is worked vertically from top to bottom. Work the pouch down the left side and half way across the bottom. Then work the right side down and across the bottom meeting in the middle of the bottom.

Bring your needle up at A and insert needle at B, directly opposite A, leaving 4 fabric threads in between. Re-emerge at C slightly lower (3 fabric threads) than A and, B and halfway between. Loop the thread under the needle and pull thread through in a downward motion. Hold thread firmly with thumb. The first stitch is completed.

Feather Stitch

CANDLE WRAP

Sibbel would have had the pleasure of stitching candle wraps for her new employer, as these were signs of wealth. Candles in homes would have been very different from the precious little stubs they would have had in the orphanage.

Materials

Fabric:

  9" x 21" piece 28 count Wichelt Natural Brown Linen (14 count Natural Brown Aida). Fabric should fit a 3" x 15" candle.

Fiber:

  Brandy (DMC 422) [/]
  Baked Clay (DMC 612) [□]
  Flax (DMC 613) [x]
  Buttermilk (DMC 677) [+]
  Old Blue Paint (DMC 926) [·]
  DMC 3768 [–]
  DMC #12 Perle Coton, Ecru

Stitches

Cross Stitch over 2 fabric threads with 2 strands of floss
Backstitch over 2 fabric threads with 2 strands of Old Blue Paint
Nun Stitch

Instructions

Measure linen and cut to fit around candle. Center Tree of Life on linen. Leave 28 threads on each side. Cross Stitch Tree with Tulips on left and Tree with Birds and Grapes on right. Keep bottom of trees even.

Finishing Instructions

Do Nun Stitch around edge of linen using 1 strand of #12 Perle Coton. To finish this wrap, you can lace back and forth with the thread or with a ribbon.

Note: When Nun Stitch is completed, remove the first non-stitched linen thread on all four sides. This is where you will cut away the excess fabric.

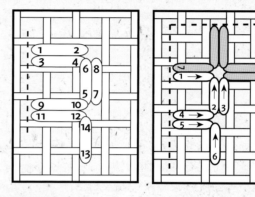

Nun Stitch

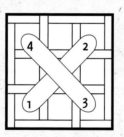

Cross Stitch over 2

Backstitch over 2

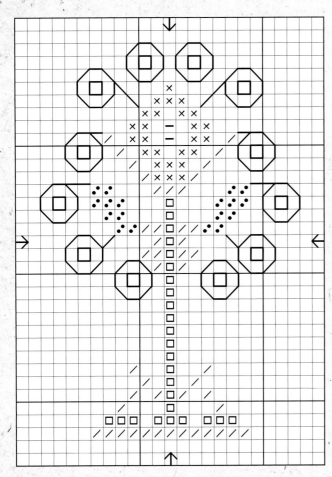

Tree of Life
Design size: 21W x 31H

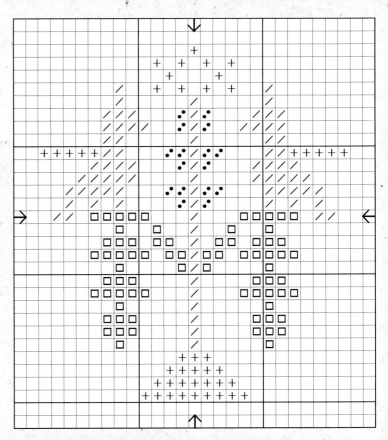

Tree with Birds and Grapes
Design size: 25W x 28H

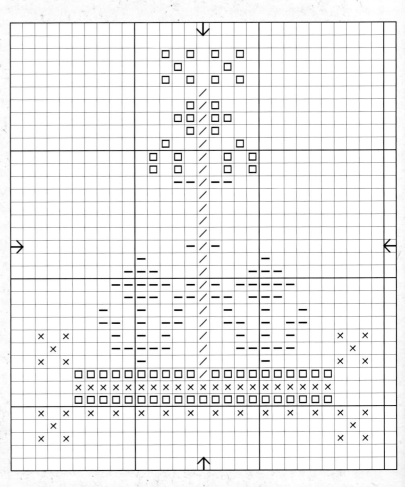

Tree with Tulips
Design size: 27W x 31H

MATTRESS PIN CUSHION

This type of pin cushion was very popular. You could do a bit of embroidery on the top and then add your pins into the sides. The colors used for this pin cushion were used sparingly in Sibbel's sampler. This was a perfect design to showcase them.

Materials

Fabric:

Two pieces measuring 6" x 10", 28 count Wichelt Natural Brown Linen (14 count Natural Brown Aida)

Additional Supplies:

18" Twill Tape, ¾" Wide
Fiberfill

Fiber:

Brandy (DMC 422) [/]
Highland Heather (DMC 778) [z]
DMC 3362 [s]

Stitches

Cross Stitch over 2 fabric threads using 2 strands of floss

Instructions

Center Cross Stitch.

Finishing Instructions

Counting out from the edge of your stitching, withdraw the 17th thread on all sides. Do the same for the back piece of linen.

Fold the raw edges to the inside. Sew twill tape with small tacking stitches to these withdrawn thread gussets. Do this for three sides of the cushion.

Stuff the cushion with fiberfill. On the last side of the cushion, fold one raw edge of twill to cover the beginning edge. Sew shut. Place pins on side as would have been done in Sibbel's time to preserve the needlework.

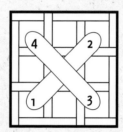

Cross Stitch over 2

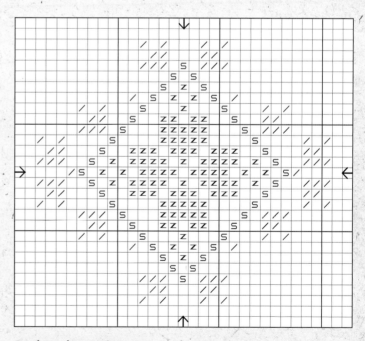

Design size: 29W x 25H

Materials

Fabric:
   2 pieces of 6" x 10" 28 count Wichelt Natural
   Brown Linen (14 count Natural Brown Aida)

Additional Supplies:
   Miscellaneous Lace: 1 yard of 2 ½"-wide lace
   for edge and 8" of ¼"-wide lace for inside trim

   Buttons: 3 large, 2 small

   Fat Quarter 18" x 22" complementary fabric
   Fiberfill

Fiber:
   Baked Clay (DMC 612) [□]
   Flax (DMC 613) [x]
   Old Blue Paint (DMC 926) [··]
   Woodrose (DMC 975) [♥]
   DMC 3768 [–]
   #12 Perle Coton

Stitches

Cross Stitch over 2 fabric threads using 2
   strands of floss
Feather Stitch

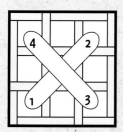

Cross Stitch over 2

Instructions

Cross Stitch over 2 threads with 2 strands.

Note: This is the Tree with Tulips stitched 3 times
using different color combinations. Find center.
Measure 4" to the left and stitch left-side tree. Leave
8 threads and stitch the center tree. Leave 8 threads
and stitch the right-side tree.

Finishing Instructions

Front Finishing: Cut the 8" of ¼" lace into two 4"
strips. To the left side of the stitching (there should
be 8 threads between the edge of the left-hand tree
and the edge of the lace), secure each of the 4"
strips of the 8" of lace using the Feather Stitch. Use 2
strands of Woodrose (DMC 975) to do this. Sew 3 large
buttons on top of the inside of the lace edges. Sew
2 small buttons between the bottom designs of the
trees. Sew buttons on with #12 Perle Coton.

Assembly

Cut a 1-yard strip by 1 ½" of finishing fabric. Begin
at the top left edge and sew strip down. Cut and
press seam to outside edge. Lay strip on previous
fabric, right side, and sew, cut, and iron. Do across
the bottom, in the same manner, and then do the
left side. Lay the 2 ½"-wide lace on the right sides,
along the raw edge of finishing fabric. Sew in place,
mitering corners. Cut a piece of finishing fabric for
the back of sewing weight. This piece should be the
same size as the entire front section. Put right sides
together, and sew the pieces together, being careful
of the lace. Leave a 2" seam. Turn inside out and stuff
with fiberfill. Hand stitch the bottom closed.

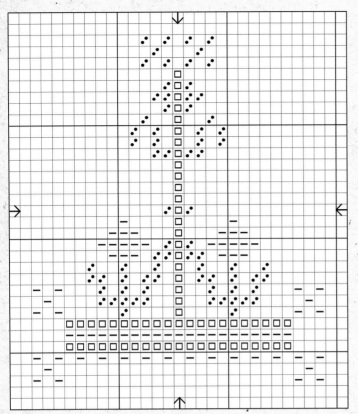

Design size: 27W x 31H

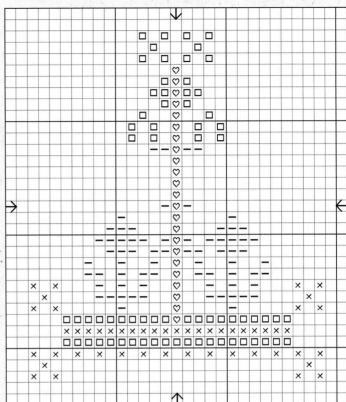

Design size: 27W x 31H

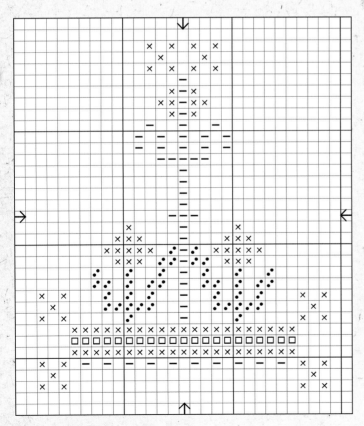

Design size: 27W x 31H

PERSONALIZATION

Use this alphabet to personalize your sampler and projects.

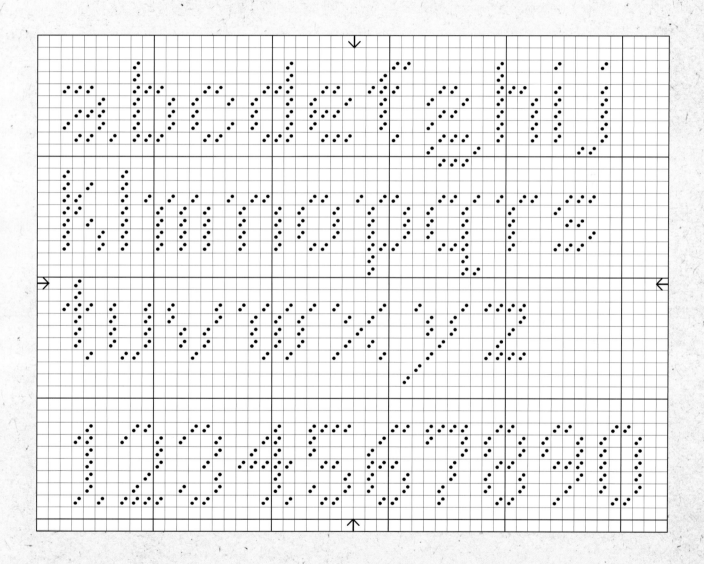

Materials

Fabric:

28 count Wichelt Natural Brown Linen (14 count Natural Brown Aida) in the following sizes:

5" x 2 ½" for "Sewing Roll"

4" x 2" for "Buttons"

4" x 1 ½" for "Needles"

3" x 2" for "Pins"

Fiber:

Brandy (DMC 422) [✓]

Finishing Materials:

15" x 5 ½" of Weeks Dye Works Wool Felt #1110HT Parchment

25" x 5 ½" complementary cotton fabric

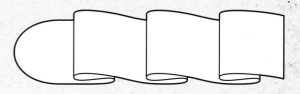

Stitches

Cross Stitch over 2 fabric threads using 2 strands of floss

Instructions

Cross-Stitch your pocket "names" over 2 threads with 2 strands of floss. Center the words "buttons," "needles," and "pins."

Cross Stitch "sewing roll" over 2 threads with 2 strands of floss.

Finishing Instructions

Remove 4 or 5 threads from the cut edge to fray the edges of your stitched "buttons," "needles," "pins" and "sewing roll" pieces.

Sew your Cross Stitched piece "sewing roll" onto the wool felt on the front.

Fold the cotton to form 3 equal pockets. See the diagram. Because the cotton is 10" larger, the pockets are 3 ½" deep. You can vary this size according to your needs. Stitch each of your Crossed Stitched pieces (buttons, needles, and pins) to folds before sewing the edges together. Refer to the drawing for guidance.

Assembly

Sew your wool and cotton pieces together.

Helpful Hint: To sew wool and cotton together, it is best to sew the cotton on top and the wool on the bottom because the wool tends to stretch under the sewing machine foot.

Iron flat.

Lay the two pieces together (right sides together) and round off the top of the wool felt and the cotton (folded with pockets) and stitch the edges together. Leave an opening at the bottom for turning. Turn and hand stitch the bottom closed.

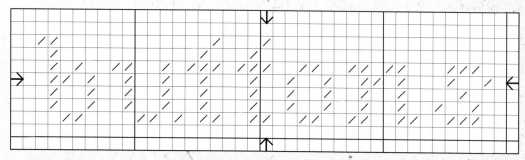

Design size: 37W x 7H

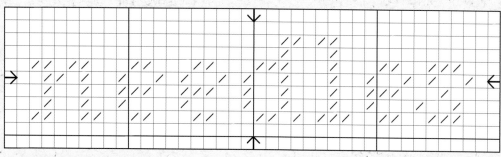

Design size: 36W x 7H

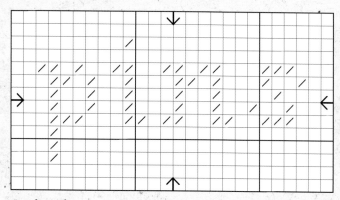

Design size: 22W x 10H

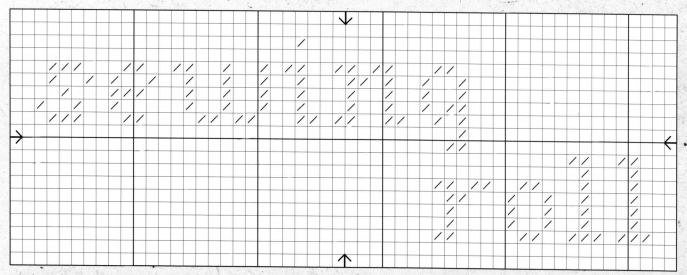

Design size: 50W x 16H

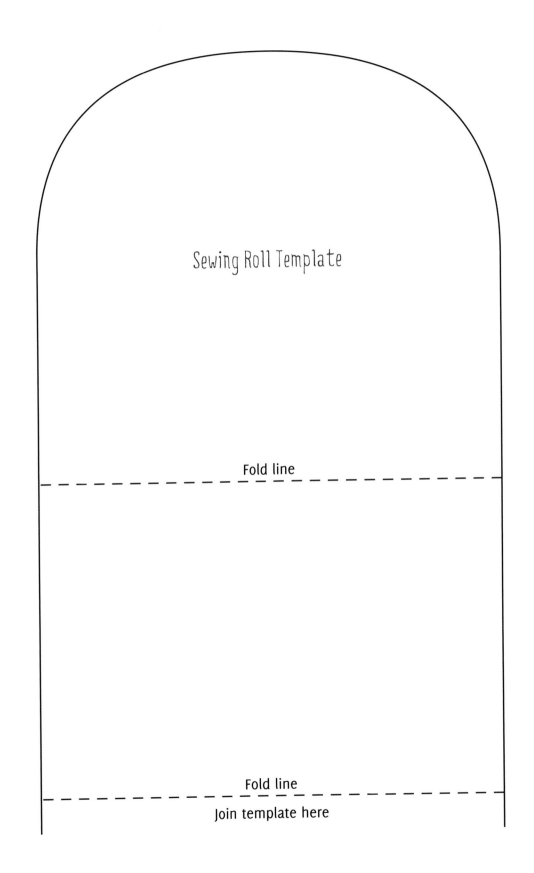

Sewing Roll Template

Fold line

Fold line

Join template here

Join template here

Fold line

POCKET PURSE

Sibbel would have worn this pocket purse under her skirt to hold her few coins when she went out to work. The pattern is a tracing of a child's purse from the Charleston Museum in South Carolina.

Materials

Fabric:
   9" x 10" piece 28 count Wichelt Natural Brown Linen (14 count Natural Brown Aida)

Additional Supplies:
   Fat Quarter 18" x 22" complementary fabric

Fiber:
   Brandy (DMC 422) [╱]
   Old Blue Paint (DMC 926) [·]
   Woodrose (DMC 975) [♥]
   DMC 3768 [−]

Stitches

Cross Stitch over 2 fabric threads using 2 strands of floss

Backstitch over 2 fabric threads using 2 strands of floss

Instructions

Measure down 4 ½". Center Cross Stitch. Backstitch the apples using 2 strands of Brandy.

Finishing Instructions

Make a pattern similar to the finished shape. Trace the pattern onto the linen. Cut away linen to leave a ½" allowance for seam. Cut a 3" slit down in top center of linen. Trace the same pattern on the fat quarter and cut out one piece, minus the slit. Sew right side of linen to right side of fabric. Clip curves. Turn inside out and iron.

Slit Binding: To make the binding for the 3" slit: Cut a piece of the fat quarter 5" long x 1" wide. Fold ¼" seams on both edges and hand sew to the slit.

Top Binding: Cut a 1" wide x 10" long piece of the fat quarter. Fold ¼" seams on both edges and hand stitch onto the linen.

To make the waist ties: Cut a 1" x 26" piece of fabric from the fat quarter and sew right sides together. Turn inside out. Tie knots in both ends. Tack on the back of the pocket.

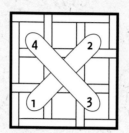

Cross Stitch over 2

Backstitch over 2

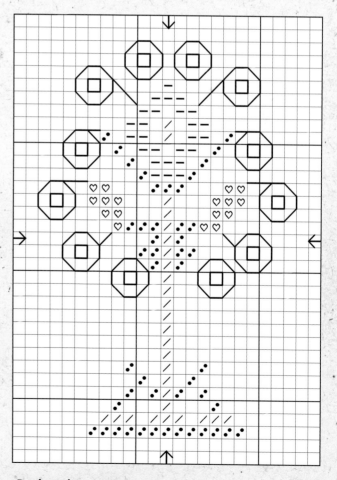

Design size: 21W x 31H

Stitch Diagrams

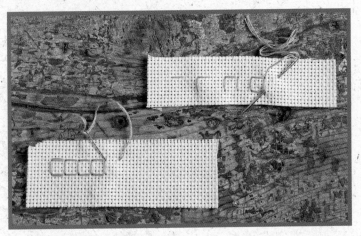

4 Sided Stitch

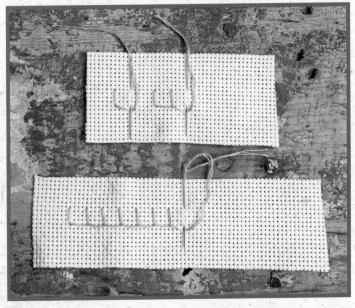

Blanket Stitch

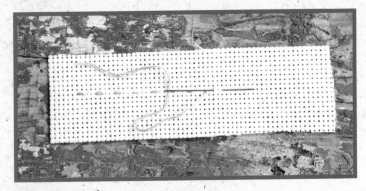

Running Stitch

Hem Stitch

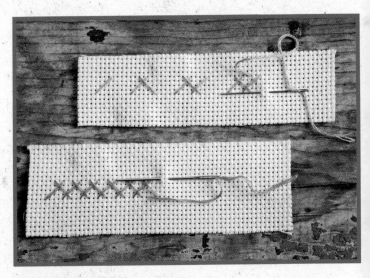

Herringbone Stitch

Feather Stitch

Bibliography

Meulenbelt-Nieuwburg, Albarta. *Embroidery Motifs from Old Dutch Samplers.*
Amsterdam: H. J. W. Becht's Uitgeversmaatschappij B.V., 1974.

Vincent, Caroline. *Sampler Workbook: Motifs & Patterns.* London: A & C
Black Publishers Ltd, 2010.

Colby, Averil. *Samplers.* London: Batsford Ltd., 1964.

Hickmott, Mary. *New Stitches No. 12.* UK: Creative Crafts
Publishing Ltd, 1994.

Nielsen, Edith. *Scandinavian Embroidery, Past and Present.* New York:
Charles Scribner's Sons, 1978.

Winter, Adalee. *Religious Designs for Needlework.* Birmingham, Ala.:
Oxmoor House, Inc., 1977.

Resources

The Gentle Art: thegentleart.com	*wholesale only*
Weeks Dye Works: weeksdyeworks.com	*wholesale only*
Wichelt Imports: wichelt.com	*wholesale only*
DMC USA: dmc-usa.com	*wholesale-retail*
Zweigart: zweigartfabric.com	*wholesale only*

Contact Still Stitching with Susan LLC for information on
wonderful classes, retreats, lectures and escapes:
www.susangreeningdavis.com

Susan Greening Davis
sgreeningd@aol.com

Sally Criswell
sallyxstitch@mindspring.com

Join Susan and Sally on their needlework retreats and historical journeys in
the United States and abroad.

still stitching with sibbel